Verses United

The Poetry of Football
Edited by Ian Horn

Illustrated by Robert Nancollis

COUNTY DURHAM BOOKS

CONTENTS

Foreword	*Bobby Robson*	4
Introduction	*Melvyn Bragg*	6
Editor's Note	*Ian Horn*	10

PART ONE: The North East

Red and White Days	*Ian Horn*	12
Beginnings (circa, 1879)		
Largo		
The People's Saturday	*Ian Horn*	14
Divisions	*Tony Harrison*	17
Travelling Fan	*Tom Pickard*	18
Angels Playing Football	*Keith Armstrong*	21
Ash	*Michael Kirkup*	22
Valediction	*Leonard Barras*	24
Come on you Reds	*Andy Croft*	25
The Wolverhampton Wanderer	*Michael Horovitz*	26

PART TWO: Home and Away

Late Evening Soccer at Rugby	*Philip Radmall*	28
Daddy Edgar's Pools	*Mike Harding*	29
Script from Liverpool v Manchester City, Christmas 1992		
	Stuart Hall	31
Death of a Football Club	*Mal Cieslak*	33
The Heart lies Low and Heavy	*Arthur Appleton*	35
The Football Replays	*Wes Magee*	36
Ball Girl		
Hwyl		

The big drop

Could Go Down	*Andy Davenport*	39
True Colours	*Henry Normal*	40
A Heart with Two Left Feet	*Henry Normal*	42
The Bell	*Adrian Henri*	43
Auntie and Italia '90	*Brendan Cleary*	44
World Cup 1990	*Linda France*	45
The Perfect Match	*Liz Loxley*	46
Cream of the Scum	*Tom Pickard*	47
Home Game	*David Stephenson*	49
Brentford versus Bristol Rovers, December 1986		
	Chris Powici	50
The Long Ball	*Robert Etty*	53
When Wembley was a Dream	*David Trembath*	56
Night Match, Ashton Gate	*Andy Reeves*	58
A Game of Two Halves	*Kevin Cadwallender*	60
Sport Story of a Winner	*Glyn Maxwell*	61
Tale of the Crimson Team	*Glyn Maxwell*	63
..... And Smith must Score!	*Attila the Stockbroker*	69
The Good Thief	*Tom Leonard*	71
From Unrelated Incidents - (4)	*Tom Leonard*	72
Nil Nil	*Don Paterson*	73
Acknowledgements		76

FOREWORD

As one who can recall Len Shackleton's first game for Newcastle United and who used to be the first in the queue to enter St James' Park, it is a particular pleasure to be asked to write the introduction for this anthology of football poetry with its strong leanings towards my native North East.

As I scribble these notes the memories come flooding back. I remember how my father, a miner whose meagre financial resources were stretched to the absolute limit, would somehow save enough each fortnight to treat myself and my brothers. How we looked forward to those 17-mile journeys from our home in Langley Park, Co. Durham, to see Newcastle play!

Shackleton's first game? It was against Newport County on October 5, 1946, Newcastle won 13-0 and he scored six. I was 13 at the time and they were all heroes to me - 'Wor' Jackie Milburn, Joe Harvey, Charlie Wayman, Bob Cowell etc. - and that result may never be superceded as the Magpies' record victory.

However , before I'm accused of being biased in a certain direction, let me acknowledge the part played by Sunderland in projecting the North East as one of the most fervent and passionate football areas in the entire world.

The mischievous Shackleton - remember how he earned the nickname Clown Prince of Soccer? - switched from St James' Park to reserve his place in the Roker hall of fame alongside other idols like Willie Watson, Billy Elliott, Charlie Hurley and the heroes of 1973 who produced a stunning Wembley triumph at the expense of Leeds United to carry off the FA Cup.

As one who has been totally immersed in football for as long as I can remember, it comes as no surprise that people are sufficiently moved to say it in verse. The great Pele called it the beautiful game - to put it another way, poetry in motion.

Bobby Robson

INTRODUCTION

They got to the football ground with a quarter of an hour to spare. Nicholas - bold to a fault- paid the taxi to stay and wait for them, partly because he was convinced that he would never be able to raise another taxi in the darkness which would follow the game, partly because the heaviness of the police presence and the crush of supporters suggested that he might badly need a line of escape.

It was the first time he had been to a major football match. This was a derby game, two of the great northern First Division teams lined up against each other. The mounted police, the circling helicopter, the growl and thrust of the crowd along from the stand entrance, moving in unsteady fat conga lines to the body-narrow turnstiles were all outside his experience. He rather prided himself on being English, but this was a mass section of, largely, English male life which was totally outside his ken. His own constituency boasted no football team that he needed to court and the few glimpses of the game on television had not prepared him for this. This was the nineteenth-century racecourse; the sixteenth-century London apprentices; Wat Tyler's peasant army; the circus of the streets - his mind flew straight into a romantic pageant of England which stirred him, moved him, both emotions heightened by a certain apprehension. Not for himself - Nicholas was a man of indisputable physical courage - but for Harry.

Harry loved it. He could have been bred for the crowd. As they climbed the stairs inside the large stand to find their seats in the upper east block, Harry held Nicholas's hand, but Nicholas was not sure who was leading when the small boy wriggled through the push and crush of men with the comfort of one to the manner born. Nicholas's well-developed courtesies were largely super-numerary.

Their Block - Block D - was on the top of what had, to Nicholas's eye, much in common with the more usual connotations of the Block system. His constituency did contain a large Victorian prison and the shoddy, cheap, cream-painted brickwork, the tramp of feet, the Blocks brought out more than a whiff of comparison. They came to a shop. Harry was perfect in this regard and Nicholas had come to love the boy's modesty. He had not quite spotted the element of desolate pessimism. It was abundantly clear that the grotto of football jerseys, shirts, socks, boots, balls, photographs, programmes, badges, scarves of several shades and varieties of wording, and surreal extensions of memorabilia, with its attendant display of monster chocolate bars, crisps, nuts, sweets and gum, was not a sight any boy could pass by without a second glance. Yet by neither a tug nor a flirt of the eye did he hint that a treat might be in order. Nicholas did not hesitate but stopped, queued, and came away with one scarf with "Champions" and the date printed on, one cap in club colours, one shirt ditto which the lady assistant said he would grow into, a very large Mars bar, a can of Coca-Cola, and a programme. Thus furnished they entered the stadium.

The pitch was so green that Nicholas reached for the word emerald. In the middle of the grey slush, barrack-bricked city over- loomed by low-bellied snow clouds, it was like a magical Persian carpet.
"Underground heating," Harry explained proudly, his wonder-struck eyes shifting over the ground like a sniper's sights. It was the first time he had ever been to any game bigger than a scrappy contest in the local park.

They sat down. Harry was on the edge of his seat and

there he stayed; now and then he would turn to Nicholas and give or rather emit from some inner core of deep rock gratitude such a beam of happiness that Nicholas all but swayed at the force of it. The boy also conducted an intermittent commentary of encouragement.

The home side was his favourite team and when the favourite players in his favourite team got the ball, a litany of prayers and exhortations issued. "Come on . . . Don't let him tackle you . . . pass . . . brilliant . . . oh *please* . . . brilliant . . . oh oh! . . . watch out! watch *out!*..."

Nicholas sat back. He did not feel as out of place as he had anticipated. They were in the most expensive seats of the stand, a few rows behind the directors' box, and he was relieved to see that there was a large number of large, well-wadded, uncheaply over-coated men, some smoking cigars, some with small boys, none conforming to the football hooligan type which characterised the football crowd in the newspapers read by Nicholas. Indeed he wondered if he had strayed into a different game. But no, the two teams came out, music played, the large men leapt up to applaud, just as excited in their overcoated way as the younger men standing on the terraces at either end behind the goalposts who then took up the major part of Nicholas's attention: the lads standing on the terraces.

He was fascinated by them.

Their chanting, always rhythmic, sometimes deafening, occasionally rude, invariably rumbustious, boomed across the ground, often echoed or challenged by supporters of the other team and sometimes accompanied by the co-ordinated waving of the arm or other gestures which he found exhilarating in their precision. The police, yellow-jacketed, were placed like Roman walls between opposing Picts and Brits and, scan as he could, Nicholas saw not a ripple of "trouble". Of course, he realised, he could have been fortunate on the day or the "trouble" - the fighting between rival supporters - could now be located outside the ground or even (as he was to discover when he pursued the matter later) have shifted away from the game altogether. But the lack of it-given the game's association with hooligan behaviour- relaxed him.

This chanting. It was tribal, that much was easy - two tribes on ancient hills provoking each other to battle. It was also, he concluded, deeply humorous, a big daft joke, a happy expression of mayhem. It pretended to be intimidating from time to time but that soon petered out and the applause for a particular player or the generalised baying for victory would start somewhere deep in the stacked terraces and suddenly electrify ten thousand, fifteen, twenty thousand throats. The numbers were themselves impressive, Nicholas thought. These were the foot-soldiers, the cannon-fodder, the boys become men on frozen fields sent to rule and destroy and uphold, lashed together now in a common voice.

As the game rattled away and Harry's team moved towards a two-goal victory, Nicholas found himself increasingly immersed in the crowd and in the sensations and thoughts it set off. The force of it! Could it ever be - at such a size - as reliably friendly as it seemed? He dived into comparisons - the men in Nelson's fleet, the men on the Western Front, the Jarrow Marchers . . . it was in a mood of rather sentimental euphoria that he left the stadium - or rather was all but carried along bodily by the satisfied crowd.

Melvyn Bragg

EDITOR'S NOTE

I hope that this selection will illustrate why the game of football matters and why people care about the game. The North East of England has produced many of the best footballers and intensely loyal supporters. There is a unique passion and obsession. This relationship goes beyond sport - it is a need to love something.

Contributions have not only come from the North East but also from outside the region, from well-known writers as well as new poets. Our national game is a common experience. A soccer team can have an impact on any community.

My own interest in football is wrapped up in my feelings about my father, about Sunderland, about my past. This book is dedicated to all of those with hope in their hearts who support the beautiful game.

Ian Horn
County Durham, 1993

PART ONE

The North East

RED AND WHITE DAYS

BEGINNINGS (circa, 1879)

At first, a team of teachers
on the Blue House field
Then a 'team of all the talents'
like J.E. Doig, 'Prince of Goalkeepers'
Players from Scotland, jobs in the shipyards.

Ian Horn

LARGO (Barnsley versus Sunderland, 1991)

The away supporters
taunted the home fans
with several verses of
* Largo, New World Symphony.

It wasn't out of place
in scenes of traditional Yorkshire folklore.
The pre-war football stadium, the colliery,
the terraced houses and
the municipal bowling green.

The away fans
echoed to a home defeat
and beyond
into a football landscape.

(* Largo by Dvořák. 'Coming Home' theme for Hovis)

Ian Horn

THE PEOPLE'S SATURDAY

In metamorphosis
the womb was a case ball.
A football sixth sense,
learned from generations
in mines, shipyards, and factories.
At the end of a working week
to follow the flow of a sub-culture, and
to be seen at the park
on the edge of town.
To witness artistry
skills beyond their workplace
Our fathers would tell us.

The modern game is a nil, nil.
Today, Gabbiadini missed, a woeful sight
this takes the Garibaldi!
No Shackleton or Carter these days
But Radio 5
And still, Mancunian romanticism
a voice that says;
'read by James Alexander-Gordon'
and reassuringly, I know,
it's another
British Saturday.

Ian Horn

To my dad,
who took me
to my first
football match.

Billy Horn
(1926 - 1991)

DIVISIONS

All aggro in tight clothes and skinhead crops,
assuming like themselves I'm on the dole,
once in the baths, that mask of 'manhood' drops,
their decorated skins lay bare their soul:

Teen age dole-wallah piss-up, then tattoos.
Brown Ale and boys' bravado numb their fright—
MOTHER in ivy, blood reds and true blues
against that North East skin so sunless white.
When next he sees United lose a match,
his 'bovvers' on, his scarf tied round his wrist,
his rash NEWCASTLE RULES will start to scratch,
he'll aerosol the walls, then go get pissed . . .

So I hope the TRUE LOVE on your arms stays true,
the MOTHER on your chest stays loved not hated.

But most I hope for jobs for all of you—

next year your tattooed team gets relegated!

Tony Harrison

TRAVELLING FAN

The train rocks
a ten year old boy,
with glasses
and scraggy red hair,
to sleep.

He counts the cooling ovens;
they're all around,
a forest of smoking towers.

His white bag with blue letters:
    LEEDS UNITED
  and in gold,
THE CHAMPIONS!

Is that your team?
Aye! who'd you support, Newcastle?
I don't suppose you want to talk
about last Saturday!

I didn't.

Tom Pickard

ANGELS PLAYING FOOTBALL

(in memory of Jackie Milburn)

Sprinkle my ashes on St. James's Park,
fragments of goals on the grass.
Hear the Gallowgate roar in the dark.
All of my dreams came to pass.

Pass me my memories,
pass me the days,
pass me a ball and I'll play:

play with the angels,
play on their wings,
play in the thunder and lightning.

I leave you these goals in my will,
snapshots of me on the run.
I leave you these pieces of skill,
moments of me in the sun.

Pass me my memories,
pass me the days,
pass me a ball and I'll play:

play with the angels,
play on their wings,
play in the thunder and lightning.

Keith Armstrong

ASH

During the bitter 1926 Miner's Strike, men from Ashington collieries helped to lay a football pitch at the Hirst Welfare by carting mountains of ash from a nearby tip. It soon became one of the finest grounds in the area.

Then, ash,
once hewed as coal
from the rich Main Seam,
lay on the tip,
like scattered dust
from an old man's dream.

Now, filled into sacks,
hoyed into barrows,
hauled to the Welfare
by young Geordie
and his striking marras;
to be spread by pitmen
with shovels of steel.

Soon, young blades of grass,
would sprout, knit together,
bonded as one,
to rise like a Phoenix
from out of the ash.

Michael Kirkup

VALEDICTION

Excerpt from 'Up the Tyne in a Flummox'

The skipper of Wallsend Amnesia football team retired in 1933 at the age of fifty-seven. He had served the club well, having sustained broken glasses on six occasions. The following tribute, penned by Herbert Mangle, the Wallsend neo-Wordsworthian poet (1882-1965), appeared in the Wallsend Weekly Buffoon:

A long farewell to all thy greatness, football friend,
Whose many goals have stirred the Tuscan ranks;
But since thou oft-times scored them through thine own team's end,
Then let us add: For this relief, much thanks!

Leonard Barras

COME ON YOU REDS

(For the Boro)

The winter tilts towards late afternoon
As the pitch soaks up the first rain, the last light.
Standing up here in the Holgate End
Good humoured, foul-mouthed, and always right,
Self-mockery keeps the cold out. A cartoon
Working-class, that forgot how to defend

And never knew how to attack. So many
Defeats. But still the floodlights gild the pitch
With flame, and something's still at stake :
A consciousness of sorts - but which ?
A glorious, phosphorous epiphany -
It's Stuart Ripley on the break !

It's the triumph of numbers, to find
A geometric increase in the slow
Arithmetic click through the turnstiles of class,
Bare-headed unity, alfresco,
Difference suspended just for a while, mind,
Among dreams of cheering, dreams of grass.

The surge of gender's limitations
Hard to resist when Slaven scores,
Held in too long, like self- like crowd-control.
And week-days, the silent stand still roars
With the reproach of generations :
'All we are saying, is give us a goal.'

Andy Croft

THE WOLVERHAMPTON WANDERER

Excerpt in which the Arsenal, Wolverhampton and Middlesbrough teams of 1948-52 are recalled.

...Dream-machine of a team –
Each man a Genius, each content – for
'Modest in Victory, Cheerful in Defeat' to be obscene
   To be Seen I mean – a small but gaily gleaming cog

   Even where, in wet or midwinter season
   The bed lay rampled to a murky bog
   – Or frosted over – hard as glacier-ramparts –
They'd brace themselves,
      Wolf Mannioned as the Nordic Middlesburghers,
   In most likewise hard and strongboned harmony –
   Erect through storm, and failure of omened truth-to-
form
   – Like as if they were
Not London's gunmen grappling wild-wolves
   – Not eleven men at all
      But co-ordinated limbs of One Man
      Labouring as 'twere
                              in every Prime of Wife.

Michael Horovitz

PART TWO

Home and Away

'Rimbaud wanted to write about everything, to seek flashes of inspiration, to enjoy different ideas and to live with different philosophies.
He had the spontaneity of a child, and I believe in that.'

Eric Cantona (Manchester United) on the French poet, Arthur Rimbaud

LATE EVENING SOCCER AT RUGBY

Across the old playing-fields,
between the ancient hedges,
the last scattered spores
blew over the cold ground, sodden
and supplicant after the dull rain.
Small, stiff bodies hacked against the gale
blowing from the broad, exposed back
of a ridge rising out of shallow valleys
dim and distant in the late gloom,
and ran through the foul weather shouting
out in the bare field,
as the ball blew away downwind into the trees,
carried, like a seed, toward the black barks
and resting art amongst acorns, conkers, dead pollen,
wet leaves cold as carrion,
going old in the damp, mossy ditch.
Then it was kicked back towards the players
wandering in the worsening murk
against the low hills
darkening around them -
until someone handled it,
deliberately, picked it up,
holding it to him, and ran with it
nursed in his arms like a large, generic spore,
germinating into another sport
across the small school ground.
And the hunched, black earth turned
towards a new season, and plunged back
into another night.

Philip Radmall

DADDY EDGAR'S POOLS

Each week you, Thursday Millionaire, would conjure up
The juju, stab the coupon with a pin
Or read the cups, perm my age and height
With Hitler's birthday and the number of
The bus that passed the window and the clump
Of pigeons on the next door neighbour's loft.
With rabbit's foot, white heather, and wishbone
You fluenced the coupon that I ran to post.

Each muggy Saturday you sat still while the set
Called out into the hushed room where I sat
With burning ears and heard a London voice
Call names as strange as shipping forecasts through the air:
Hamilton Academicals, Queen of the South,
Pontefract United, Hearts of Midlothian,
Wolverhampton Wanderers, Arbroath, Hibernian,
And once, I thought, a boy called *Patrick Thistle.*

Then every week after the final check,
When Friday's dreams were scratched out with a squeaky pen,
You took down from upstairs your brass band coat,
Gave me the wad of polish and the button stick.
And there in that still, darkened room I polished up
Each brassy button world that showed my face;
While you on shining tenor horn played out
Your Thursday Millionaire's lament
For a poor man's Saturday gone.

Mike Harding

SCRIPT FROM LIVERPOOL v MANCHESTER CITY, CHRISTMAS 1992

Bitterly cold at the Colosseum, must be - John Barnes wore red tights and black gloves. Even chillier for Wright, Stewart and Thomas - dropped by Caesar Souness in his quest for the Golden Fleece - the championship. So with two ScandoVikings at the back - Piechnik and Bjornebye battle was joined. City took a 30 minute buffeting, the ball zooming over the bar - Coton living dangerously, City's back four impressive. Phelan and Earle fast and flashy. Andy Hill resolute, steadfast Liverpool tho' were playing a naive offside game sprung twice by City. Flitcroft as his name implies is a flitter of a footballer - he flits into space with invention but he smote a post.

White *scored* - no offside.

Then 42 minutes Brightwell and Sheron down the right - the ball whipped in - Niall Quinn headed past a flailing Mike Hooper. Nil - one at half time.

Five minutes into the 2nd half at last a Liverpool move of sweet simplicity. Jones out wide to MacManaman - 1st time low cross - Ian Rush's stunning electric volley. The game white hot.

As you all know the modern game is all youth, pace, and movement. So into the fray steps Peter Reid the venerable warrior. Pepper and salt hair, legs so battered and bent they should be on Eastbourne seafront in a bath-chair. I had visions of the trainer abandoning the magic sponge and rushing forth with a zimmer frame.

Alongside Reid - Steve McMahon a mobile gun emplacement. He dismembered Ian Rush - yellow card. He disembowelled Redknapp - the referee merely grimaced and gave succour to Redknapp. At the whistle the City fans applauded Steve - the Kop cheered him off. Reidie and Macker - youth in its prime.

Stuart Hall
Sports Report, BBC Radio 5

DEATH OF A FOOTBALL CLUB

(Aldershot F. C. 1926-1992)

As an old faithful
he'd been here for every game.
Sixty solid years,
and then this grief
that brings a harsh, ensuing wind
around the ground
as men in reluctant suits
prepare his coffin.

More proud undaunted ghosts
glide across the pitch
towards the East Bank stand.
Memories of Melia, Howarth.
A courteous shroud
hovering where the floodlights
gleamed and flickered. Memories
of Charlton, Best, the Shots one up!

Dads who came as children
with their dads
mourning their lost Saturdays
and a thousand other friends.
Reality forms its own courtege:
circumstances of guilt and suspicion,
a climate no one
wished to comprehend.

But now just as we feared
there is an end,
a bitter tear that reaches from the heart
at this strange funeral.
A moment
when the stillness is complete
and all that's left
are memories.

Mal Cieslak

THE HEART LIES LOW AND HEAVY

The heart lies low and heavy
The legs have turned to stone,
The knowing doctor probes and tests
With every device known.

Blood pressure is all right, he says,
The blood supply is perfect,
Muscular strength is well maintained,
No congenital defect.

Bacteria is innocent,
Then he confirms his station,
The cause, he says, is obvious,
It's known as relegation.

Arthur Appleton

THE FOOTBALL REPLAYS

'Football in England is a grey game played on grey days for grey people.' Rodney Marsh

Ball girl

A pre-match bonus
she runs onto the pitch
wearing white shorts, red shirt,
and toe-punts a ball
towards the centre circle.

Stuff that! the thousands mutter
and then realise
that beneath her shirt
she is wearing not a thing.
Breasts bouncing loose!

Sudden in-whistle of breath
and every eye hard-on
that patch of red cloth:
a silence you could ignite
before she canters off,

legs hacking sideways,
to a growing, primitive roar.
Minutes later World War Three kicks off
and we're left with that vision;
soft flesh, unfettered, free.

Wes Magee, County Ground, Swindon

Hwyl

The final whistle imminent
　with the Swans two up
　　and arrogant.
　　　In stands and on terraces
　　　　fifteen thousand fans
　　　　are one-voiced,
　　　　　a Welsh choir
　　　　　　whose anthem
　　　　　　　rises
　　　　　　　　full-throated
　　　　　　　to the night.
　　　　　The match flows on,
　　　　a mere back-drop
　　　　to this event
　　　of greater passion.
　　A Celtic fervour
　　proclaims itself
　and the moon
inclines an ear to listen.

Wes Magee, Vetch Field, Swansea

The big drop

He has clambered
  high among
the rusted girders
  of the 'shed'
and from there views
  a Subbuteo-sized
relegation decider.
  The match is tidal
- red waves roll in,
  are repulsed,
roll in again-
  until on the hour
there is a home goal
  to celebrate.
Druid-like his hands
  praise the night.
Falling he drops
  to what?
Arms? Concrete?
  The game surges:
the fans bay at
  one hundred full moons
which glare from the
  darkness.

Wes Magee, County Ground, Swindon

COULD GO DOWN

Could go down ... that's the thing
that's just it ... could go down,
too bad that we languish from these displays
though it's just an aside
compared to inside...

The attack too intricate,
its foraging too offbeat,
defensively a ramshackle farce
playing a bottleneck system easily cracked
and me an over-precious amateur quack
realising we could go down
revealing I could go down
just the thing ... could go down ...

Tranquil surface stacks a backlog of trauma
unpredicted ... their overspill days
obsessive ... such self-centred ways
semblance of idyllic in midfield,
yet see them scatter on loss of possession,
could go down ... now that's the thing,
could go down ... without attack,
could go down ... one final fling,
could go down ... remains the crack.

Replayed days stagnate in the gut
could go down ... that's the cut ...

Andy Davenport

TRUE COLOURS

The roots of my underlying personal philosophy and my political perception could well go back to around the age of 8.

For football at Hogarth primary school we'd tend to divide roughly into red shirts versus blue shirts, but my Aunt Margaret had given me an old Blackburn Rovers shirt she'd bought cheap at a jumble (purple and black chequered).

Strangely enough I was the only kid with a Blackburn Rovers shirt, but then we did live in Nottingham which I always felt was a good test of a true Rovers supporter. Most of the other kids would naturally display allegiance to their favourite heroes Man. United, Forest or Liverpool, Man.

City or Chelsea pretending to be George Best or Rodney Marsh or whoever.

I was always Ralph Ironmonger, possibly Blackburn's finest ever left back.

What the other kids failed to recognise was that although they were committed to a definite side I still had the freedom of choice. I could play for the reds or the blues. I could even swap sides halfway through … without telling anyone. I sometimes wonder if my Aunt Margaret was secretly an anarchist.

Henry Normal

A HEART WITH TWO LEFT FEET

In the game of love
he stands out on the wing
awaiting the ball
looking dangerous
until when finally the
ball is played to his feet
he panics under pressure
and kicks the ball into touch.

Henry Normal

THE BELL

The bell
tolled all afternoon
we did not send to ask
for whom.
It told of flowers
heaped in a goalmouth,
red and blue scarves
heaped together at an altar;
it told of
eyes like T.V. screens
haunted by last night's images,
tears dried by the April wind.
As the flags at half-mast
stirred overhead
the deep bell
still tolled in our heads
long after the light had gone.

Adrian Henri

AUNTIE AND ITALIA '90

Auntie just couldn't stand
another penalty shoot-out.

She was quaking,
spreading her scones
haphazardly.

I was fisting the air
by the climax
and her apron flew up
like a banner.

Full of 'oohs and ahs'
she wanted to know
who that keeper was?

I had to rush upstairs
for her heart pills.

It's insane
now she says
she's going to be

a Chelsea supporter .....

Brendan Cleary

WORLD CUP 1990

I profess blasé distaste at any mention
of that boys'-stuff convention
of twenty-three men and a ball;
but can't deny England's penalties claimed all my attention.
How do the high and mighty fall!

Linda France

THE PERFECT MATCH

Football at its best
Is quite like sex...
All sweat and adrenalin
And choreographed movements,
A variety of positions,
Perfect ball control.

Plus the well known metaphor
For the orgasm
As the nubile striker
Scores a goal.

And to finish it off
"You'll Never Walk Alone"
A love song sung
In the afterglow.

Liz Loxley

CREAM OF THE SCUM

Its in the net!
Not quite pet.
Hero. Puddin.
You stupid gett!
What a good'n.

It's off his heed.
It's in. It's not.
He lacked speed.
What a farce.
Next time use ya arse!

It slipped off his boot
like a greased rat
up a drainpipe.

Hero. Guttersnipe.
Cream of the scum.
With a heed like that
yi should be hung.

Lovers, lovers, football brothers;
rejects, dejects, clowns and crakaz:
boot him one, in the nakaz!

He's on the floor.
Not anymore.
Get it back.
Give him a crack.
Lob it. Stop it.
Put the block on it.

Watch ya teeth
his elbows lethal.
He's trying. He's tripped.
He's flying.
Did you see him shift?
I'll buy him.

Lovers, lovers, football brothers;
rejects, dejects, clowns and crakaz:
boot him one, in the nakaz!

Tom Pickard

HOME GAME

They just weren't in the same league.
She was into First Division fatigue,
champion for the second season up,
while he got knocked out
in the preliminary bouts
of the sweet FA cup.

Funny game, love:
two players, no referee,
few rules to speak of;
the match usually a draw,
or decided by a penalty,
and nobody knows the score.

What he wanted was a world-class striker.
All she needed was for him to like her.

David Stephenson

BRENTFORD VERSUS BRISTOL ROVERS, DECEMBER 1986

9 Minutes: Rebelling against the supposed
intellectual stand-offishness
of Larkin and Hughes
Holloway's cross eludes
defence and forward line
and like a phrase from Eliot's Wasteland
Post-modernism escapes
and a goal-kick results

"Oh Merde Alors, You Silly bugger'"
the man beside me yells

I light another cigarette
and think of William Burroughs

17 Minutes: Inspired by the proletarian zeal
of the away fans
braving the soft West London rain
as if it were the final futile blows
of a terminal imperialism
Morgan puts Rovers ahead from 12 yards

The working class must always take
its opportunities

Half-Time: I read some Doris Lessing
and debate the sub-text
of Jamie Murray's haircut
with my neighbour

Time weighs heavy on our shoulders
like jumping for a ball with Micky Droy

53 Minutes: Lulled into a really rather charming posture
of Neo-cubist radical detachment
by the familiar announcement
that someone's double-parked
their Vauxhall Viva in the Ealing Road,
the Rovers' defence is caught square
by the classical simplicity
of Cooke's diagonal run
and Brentford equalise!

I forget Doris Lessing
the man beside me lights a cigarette
and we discuss Robbie Cooke
as a metaphor for the justification
of a cultural elite

87 Minutes: Brentford miss their fourteenth chance
to clinch the game and Rovers scramble
a drab disgusting pathetic tasteless
reactionary inevitable late-winner

All art is a mystery

Full Time I turn to my neighbour and we file out
like refugees from a revolution
that has failed to occur

On the way back to Chiswick
I notice that someone has written
"HOORAY FOR MEANINGLESS WORK"
on the window of a 237 Bus

I bet it's true as well

Chris Powici

THE LONG BALL
(A Midfielder hangs up his boots)

Will it be insurance now? Chanting from a *Filofax*
to couples on sofas whose eyes flick towards the clock?
Or sportswear-repping somewhere, maybe? ("Oh, you played for...
But call me next week!") There'll be my send-off — red card joke! -

on the last Saturday, waving from the centre spot
to the lads in scarves, the ticket stands and windows where
the sponsors sit, a chuck in the bath from the team,
boot-hanging-up photos, then that'll be it. Unfair,

this lark, I'm starting to think - not so much high kicking
as a professional foul! There's weekends apart from
the wife and kids, three in a room at some poky
hotel with a view over northern Birmingham;

the injuries (my shinbone's as smooth as a crocodile's
neck); mid-table nil-nils on misty nights; times when
the crowd gets on your back; the cockups - that penalty
I clobbered wide at Burnley in the Cup, missing two open

goals at Plymouth Argyle and dropping into the Fourth;
being put on the transfer list and feeling like shop-
soiled shinpads. I can't say I haven't had good times, too:
a semi-final at Goodison Park, non-stop

all the way; the Championship medal with Albion;
the goals, when you see it hit the net and they leap on
you and the shout goes up and you think you're twenty feet
tall. They tell me I'm living on a name and I cheapen

myself every time I go on and they substitute me
just past half-time. "A stabilising influence",
the manager says I am. He's the same age as me -
back four at Luton and Mansfield Town. He had the sense

to take to the bench when his old pins slowed him down,
so I'm letting him have the final, wise word:
"We'll give you a good testimonial - get a few
of the old stars down!" (My neighbour's son had heard

of just two, but he said he enjoyed the game.) It's home
against Huddersfield, my last match, the first weekend in May.
I feel I've played it now. I gaze at the photos
on the wall - that header at Sheffield Wednesday

and the long-distance shot at Stoke - and it doesn't
look like me. Sharp, these kids are, today. Too quick, too much
skill. They do what you don't expect. I'm chasing a long ball
to the sideline and it's in a skid somewhere near touch.

Robert Etty

WHEN WEMBLEY WAS
A DREAM

It was the surest way out of solitude
You just walked into a lane, kicked a ball,
The thumping rebound from foot to hedgerow
Carried a message certain as radio waves.
What began as a lonely dream of scoring the last goal
In the last second to win at some distant Wembley,
Became a running pattern of skinny, scuffling boys.
The swerve, trap, tackle, the shot, leap, goal,
Was our best, most honest mimicry of the greats
Who stared out from cigarette and chewing gum cards.

Every game was a cup final,
Only time and numbers exceeded rules,
In a match played for a jamjar filled with flowers.
All afternoon, long and into evening we chased,
Sweated, swore, tripped, kicked and never grew tired;
While the daisies, purple tufted vetch, campion
And the misty flames of sorrel stalks
Shrank and wilted in a glass jar,
Still labelled with a Robertson's golliwog,
It stood by the clothes that marked the goal.

Forty or fifty boys might have played,
Drifting in on boredom, out on errands,
At a time when children did the shopping
On tick till Friday when the men got paid.
A setting sun would cast its plum coloured light
On a scoreline of thirty seven thirty two,
When one of us would go home cup clutching,
Not caring that the flowers had died
For there were more of them in the fields
Than goals to score, or seconds to sleep

Until the next game.

David Trembath

NIGHT MATCH, ASHTON GATE

Caught up in the crowd's eager stream,
I'd be pulled by Dad's guiding hand
Towards the swelling expectant hum
Rising from the quickly filling stands

Picked out in the floodlight beams.
Climbing steps of old concrete,
Between familiar hopeful faces
We'd find the allotted wooden seats,

And clutching programme I'd settle back
Amid the grown-up pipe-smoke smells,
Drinking in the floodlit green,
Constructing the weekly woven spells;

And all this, a stew of small boy's senses
Topped by a lid of covering dark,
Endless, contrasting with the minute study
Of every action on the park.

I'd feel, then, a shared excitement,
That whatever else went on that night
Could not be as pure and true as this,
This special private, public delight.

Now, of course, the ground seems smaller
And rarely - though sometimes - quite as full;
But alone, or with adult mates
The night match still has a certain pull,

Irresistible, though not as innocent,
And not the union it once was,
Still something each time unique,
More than the game itself- perhaps because

The memory of the guiding hand
Tends to return like a spinning ball,
Reconciling to me somehow
That 'now' with all that went before.

Andy Reeves

A GAME OF TWO HALVES

A division three morning
in a division four town
a thousand footballs ago.

He was the first
black man I'd ever seen
and the terraces
didn't care only booed
when he missed a sitter
or got too greedy.

After blowing his chance
in first division reserves,
after screwing some Director's wife,
he got relegated to this turf.

Later on
in the 'pictures'
we'd see him sleeping
off the drink,
Sleeping off
the missed opportunities,
Slipping a cross
into a non-league goal.

Kevin Cadwallender

SPORT STORY OF A WINNER
(for Alun and Amanda Maxwell)

He was a great ambassador for the game.
      He had a simple name.
His name was known in households other than ours.
      But we knew other stars.
We could recall as many finalists
      as many panellists.
But when they said this was his Waterloo,
      we said it as ours too.

His native village claimed him as its own,
      as did his native town,
adopted city and preferred retreat.
      So did our own street.
When his brave back was up against the wall,
      our televisions all
got us shouting, and that did the trick.
      Pretty damn quick.

His colours were his secret, and his warm-up
      raindance, and his time up
Flagfell in the Hook District, and his diet
      of herbal ice, and his quiet
day-to-day existence, and his training,
      and never once explaining
his secret was his secret too, and his book,
      and what on earth he took

that meant-to-be-magic night in mid-November.
                        You must remember.
His game crumbled, he saw something somewhere.
                        He pointed over there.
The referees soothed him, had to hold things up.
                        The ribbons on the Cup
were all his colour, but the Romanoff
                        sadly tugged them off.

We saw it coming, didn't we. We knew
                        something he didn't know.
It wasn't the first time a lad was shown
                        basically bone.
Another one will come, and he'll do better.
                        I see him now - he'll set a
never-to-be-beaten time that'll last forever!
                        Won't he. Trevor.

Glyn Maxwell

TALE OF THE CRIMSON TEAM

For they were the leading team and they met at about
Ten this morning, and filed up into their coach.
They were known for their crimson colour, the dog on the shirt
Rampant, as they say, or 'rampant', as they said.
They had a song, and by the time
The Manager, scarved, was standing up by the Driver
And trying to wave the noise down they were singing it,
Though by the time they finished the whole
Party was out in the countryside, and the singing was
Settling back to yawns and a little silence.
Some were just about sleeping, and even the five
At the very back were smoking or looking out,
I-spying cars with crimson stars in the quarterlights,
Shocking a passenger with who they were
And how relaxed they seemed! whose favourite colour
Was known to every boy and was always crimson.
The passenger would never forget those seconds.
For the Crimson Team were the best on all of the islands,
And on their way to a distant town to prove it,
As they had proved it time and time again,
To all proud cities and the upstart towns, in
Sweat and sun, in filths and rain, at night,
In other hemispheres and another decade.
And this game? Workaday, to be honest, a chore!
Well almost, just a matter of getting there
And doing the business, as they put it. The players
Had plans for the evening, back in their own places,
Each the bull of a clubnight's foaming love,
Far from rivals and the inept defeated.

Today's opponents would play in an ivy green.
Something to do with the history of their hole,
That colour. Not exactly the Rampant Crimson,
Was it. They hadn't a snowball in hell, that shower,
Known for their sallow faces and dissent.
And they played at a rotting ground in industrial wind.
– Made the Crimson wonder why they bothered,
The Ivy Greens, when they could spend the same time
Say, fishing, out of harm's way, like good boys,
Instead of stumbling again round their own ground.
They were almost as bad as the Blue lot, that
Arrogant and hustling mob of ex-
Bootroom boys they'd humbled last week,
Or the local Pinks, exponents of the kick,
Whom they'd dutifully upended on the last
Day of the last season. Not to mention that
Brown-and-Yellow hooped and cheating gang:
Unprofessionals. The Crimson sang
The songs of the dim shame of all opponents.
They were in fine voice in the sun: it was elevenish.
The Number 1, the old hand, was back on form
With anecdotes of the knackered old heroes
They'd all grown up on. The Numbers 11 and 12
Started the usual jokes to the usual groans.
The fields went by at their pace and the hurtling road
Flew on at its faster pace. The Number 5
Looked to the faraway villages and hoped
What he always hoped, checking his bag again.
A fixed opinion struck the Number 10,
(He'd kept his aisle-seat, among so many men),
While the Number 4 suggested the game they never
Tired of playing but couldn't get it going this time:
They all seemed almost in awe

Of the brightness that flooded the coach, cresting them all
With daylight, lightening them, as if the aspect
Of their excellence was making itself visible,
Appearing as a - blond light, an admission that
None would ever better them, none *could* ever.
The Number 7, the youngster, tipped for a place
In a team to play the Rest of the World this summer,
Woke from a dream of that and broke the silence
With the question 'What's with the silence?'
And if you call this an answer the Number 3
Turned from the window and said 'This ain't the way.'
The motorway did seem empty, for a motorway:
No bridges, pylons, now no markings either.
The Manager confided to the Driver
He didn't recognise the country. The Driver
Turned to the Manager, smiled and confided
He didn't recognise the country either.
Come up on this cloud, friend - you know who you are
And this isn't forever, make yourself comfy there –
Peer down at the moving veins of the land.
You haven't the vertigo I have. I have to
Rope myself to this solider nimbus here;
But look at the traffic inching along where it is.
Does it all have someone to hate or beat or both?
You imagine so. I imagine so too.
Something to always know, always do.
The islands are lacerated with that today, that
Feeling, as if the great heat hatched it alive,
Sniffling along from its home to its enemy's.
The roads are blinding, the bare-headed sweat in the lay-by,
Directing to destinations each will duly
Scorn and spare no effort to overrun.
Loyalty will be bloody; menace fun.

Chants will be crude and easy to memorise,
There will be no arbiter, quarter or compromise,
And the victory will be bugled home as a merited
Fair ransacking - any shock, impossible loss
A falsehood or concealed. There will be no gain
That's not for good. Down the unwinding lane
Crawls that lonely coach which is following
Only it. Where is it going? Not home:
Somebody else's home to dishearten it,
Sadden its working self with a loaded luck
And leave it. It streams its colour behind it, its hour
Is only that, its colour its colour for what.
They're only games, and this is only that.
But as such, watch it with me, focus upon
The coach of the unison of hoping males,
Losing itself in this place where nothing's to play,
Where it isn't necessarily day or night-time,
Where no one will shout at odds or accuse or cheat them,
There is no plan to embarrass, blame or defeat them,
And nothing they risk will blunder into its obverse.
No,

The bright unoffended fields will be waiting, swaying,
Shushed, for the coach to come to its standstill by them;
For the Driver to shrug at the Manager, as if the
Silence of his own men was what had stopped them,
For player to glance at player and give away nothing
One could infer as fear but to turn away
Chewing, to confirm that as far as the eye could blink
Or believe were somebody's fields and the motorway
Had come to nothing there. Whose fields they were
Was nowhere to be seen.
The fields were wheatfields.
And those, further and redder with, no, poppies?

Hardly, not now. While yes, a gust of life, a
Blurring aeroplane wake, long underlining
Its white forgetting that it was ever noise.

The coach door opens and glints as they file out.
Against the numb horizon they make these plans:
Food, a party to quest for and question the first
Local they find. Number 1 to get to a phone.
If he must he will talk to men of the distant town
They came to outflank and fool. He will first say 'wait'.
He will choose his words. He will finally say 'help'.
He will gaze at the coach and its disappointed cargo.

They will don their crimson strip with the printed dogs
To show solidarity. Some will strike up the song.
The Numbers 11 and 12 will come into their own
At last as jokers, putting the Manager's scarf on
To cheers and shouts for a change. The young Number 7s
Dream will be longer and slower towards its end.
A different view will occur to the Number 10.
The Number 5 will be long-gone by then.
The Manager and the Driver will learn each other's
Histories, and from them, and those at the back
Will share what's left of the Marlboros.
                                        The wind
Will bustle its great way across the fields,
Green, yellowish, reddish fields and flutter
The hair on the forehead of every player, that wind,
And whisk the clouds in front of the setting sun,
And peel the clouds away from the rising sun
Until they are found, if they're ever found, a team
Who knew the tricks, who played in beautiful
Crissing patterns they worked on on floodlit nights

In sevens, lightning threes and incredible twos,
And never believed they would lose, and, at the last,
Believed they would never lose.

Glyn Maxwell

..... AND SMITH MUST SCORE!

Five yards out, an open goal
and not a man in sight
the memory of that awful miss
still haunts me late at night
Ten seconds left in extra time
and history in the making
but Smith's shot hit the goalie's legs
and now our hearts are breaking

A paraplegic lemming
with the skill of a dead cat
and the finesse of a hamster
could have done better than that!
A decomposing dogfish
wrapped in bondage, head to toe
could have stuck that ball into the net
but Gordon Smith? Oh, no!

When Robinson broke down the left
and put the ball across
we knew for sure the Seagulls' win
was Man. United's loss
And as old Smithy shaped to shoot
a mighty roar went up -
The impossible had happened!
WE'D WON THE F.A. CUP!

A fleeting glimpse of glory:
alas, 'twas not to be ...
we lost the replay 4-0
now we're in Division Three
The one chance of a lifetime
so cruelly snatched away
But till the white coats come for me
I'll ne'er forget that day .....

Attila the Stockbroker

THE GOOD THIEF

heh jimmy
yawright ih
stull wayiz urryi
ih

heh jimmy
ma right insane yirra pape
ma right insane yir wanny us jimmy
see it nyir eyes
wanny uz

heh

heh jimmy
lookslik wirgonny miss thi gemm
gonny miss thi GEMM jimmy
nearly three a cloke thinoo

dork init
good jobe theyve gote thi lights.

Tom Leonard

From UNRELATED INCIDENTS -(4)

sittn guzz-
lin a can
a newcastle
brown wotchn
scotsport hum-
min thi furst
movement a
nielsens thurd
symphony - happy
iz larry yi
might say;

a wuz jist turn-
in ovir thi
possibility uv
oapnin anuthir
can whin thi
centre forward
picked up
a loose baw:
hi huddiz back
tay thi
right back iz
hi caught
it wayiz in -
step n jist
faintn this way
then this
way, hi turnd
n cracked it;
jist turnd n
cracked it;
aw nwan move-
ment; in ti
thi net.

Tom Leonard

NIL NIL

Just as any truly accurate representation of a particular geography can only exist on a scale of 1:1 (imagine the vast, rustling map of Burgundy, say, settling over it like a freshly-starched sheet!) so it is with all our abandoned histories, those ignoble lines of succession that end in neither triumph nor disaster, but merely plunge on into deeper and deeper obscurity; only in the infinite ghost-libraries of the imagination - their only possible analogue - can their ends be pursued, the dull and terrible facts finally authenticated.

François Aussemain, *Pensées*

From the top, then, the zenith, the silent footage:
McGrandle, majestic in ankle-length shorts,
his golden hair shorn to an open book, sprinting
the length of the park for the long hoick forward,
his balletic toe-poke nearly bursting the roof
of the net; a shaky pan to the Erskine St End
where a plague of grey bonnets falls out of the clouds.
But ours is a game of two halves, and this game
the semi they went on to lose; from here
it's all down, from the First to the foot of the Second,
McGrandle, Visocchi and Spankie detaching
like bubbles to speed the descent into pitch-sharing,
pay-cuts, pawned silver, the Highland Division,
the absolute sitters ballooned over open goals,
the dismal nutmegs, the scores so obscene
no respectable journal will print them; though one day
Farquhar's spectacular bicycle-kick
will earn him a name-check in Monday's obituaries.
Besides the one setback - the spell of giant-killing
in the Cup (Lochee Violet, then Aberdeen Bon Accord,
the deadlock with Lochee Harp finally broken
by Farquhar's own-goal in the replay)

nothing inhibits the fifty-year slide
into Sunday League, big tartan flasks,
open hatchbacks parked squint behind goal-nets,
the half-time satsuma, the dog on the pitch,
then the Boy's Club, sponsored by Skelly Assurance,
then Skelly Dry Cleaners, then nobody;
stud-harrowed pitches with one-in-five inclines,
grim fathers and perverts with Old English Sheepdogs
lining the touch, moaning softly.
Now the unrefereed thirty-a-sides,
terrified fat boys with callipers minding
four jackets on infinite, notional fields;
ten years of dwindling, half-hearted kickabouts
leaves two little boys—Alastair Watt,
who answers to 'Forty', and wee Horace Madden,
so smelly the air seems to quiver above him -
playing desperate two-touch with a bald tennis ball
in the hour before lighting-up time.
Alastair cheats, and goes off with the ball
leaving wee Horace to hack up a stone
and dribble it home in the rain;
past the stopped swings, the dead shanty-town
of allotments, the black shell of Skelly Dry Cleaners
and into his cul-de-sac, where, accidentally,
he neatly back-heels it straight into the gutter
then tries to swank off like he meant it.

Unknown to him, it is all that remains
of a lone fighter-pilot, who, returning at dawn
to find Leuchars was not where he'd left it,
took time out to watch the Sidlaws unsheathed
from their great black tarpaulin, the haar burn off Tayport
and Venus melt into Carnoustie, igniting

the shoreline; no wind, not a cloud in the sky
and no one around to admire the discretion
of his unscheduled exit: the engine plopped out
and would not re-engage, sending him silently
twirling away like an ash-key,
his attempt to bail out only partly successful,
yesterday having been April the 1st-
the ripcord unleashing a flurry of socks
like a sackful of doves rendered up to the heavens
in private irenicon. He caught up with the plane
on the ground, just at the instant the tank blew
and made nothing of him, save for his fillings,
his tackets, his lucky half-crown and his gallstone,
now anchored between the steel bars of a stank
that looks to be biting the bullet on this one.

In short, this is where you get off, reader;
I'll continue alone, on foot, in the failing light,
following the trail as it steadily fades
into road-repairs, birdsong, the weather, nirvana,
the plot thinning down to a point so refined
not even the angels could dance on it. Goodbye.

Don Paterson

ACKNOWLEDGEMENTS

The publishers wish to thank the authors and various copyright holders for permission to include the poems reprinted in this book including the following:

Wes Magee, Leonard Barras and Robert Etty, IRON PRESS;
Tom Pickard, ALLISON AND BUSBY;
Philip Radmall NEW DEPARTURES, GRANDCHILDREN OF ALBION;
Henry Normal A TWIST IN THE TALE PUBLISHING;
Tom Leonard Intimate Voices: Writing 1965-83 GALLOPING DOG PRESS;
'Copyright Mike Harding, from Daddy Edgar's Pools (1992), reproduced by permission of PETERLOO POETS'
'Sport Story of a Winner', 'Tale of the Crimson Team', reprinted by permission of BLOODAXE BOOKS LTD. from: Out of the Rain by Glyn Maxwell (Bloodaxe Books, 1992).
'..... And Smith Must Score!' reprinted by permission of BLOODAXE BOOKS LTD. from: Scornflakes by Attila the Stockbroker (Bloodaxe Books, 1992).
'The Bell', from Wish You Were Here by Adrian Henri (Jonathan Cape Ltd, 1990; © Adrian Henri 1990). Reproduced by permission of ROGERS, COLERIDGE & WHITE LTD.
'Divisions' by Tony Harrison reprinted by permission of IRON PRESS.Reproduced by permission of PETERS, FRASER & DUNLOP LTD.
'Nil Nil' from the collection Nil Nil by Don Paterson (FABER and FABER LTD, 1993)
Introduction by Melvyn Bragg taken from 'Crystal Rooms' published by HODDER AND STOUGHTON.

The copyright of each of the poems in this volume remains with the author or the copyright holder.

Photographs

Page 11, The Sunderland team of 1931 during a surrealist period. *(Newcastle Evening Chronicle)*
Page14, Football crowd on the Wear bridge during the early fifties. *(Sunderland Echo)*
Page 15, The Sunderland captain (Horatio Carter) with Millwall's Magnall before the 1937 F.A. Cup semi-final at Huddersfield. *(Sunderland Echo)*
Page 20, Jackie Milburn, *(Arthur Appleton)*

© Ian Horn, 1993

Published by County Durham Books, 1993

ISBN 1 897585 06 3

Supported by Northern Arts and Durham County Council; Arts, Libraries and Museums Department.

George Best was always being told to stop enjoying himself. "I remember once", he says, "I woke up in a massive hotel room. There were champagne bottles all over the floor and the present Miss World was naked in my bed. An old porter came in and shook his head sadly at me. 'George, George', he said, 'where did it all go wrong?' Well, if that's going wrong ....."